EAST RIDING
OF YORKSHIRE COUNCIL

Schools Library Service

PROJECT
2018

FESTIVAL POEMS & RHYMES

CHOSEN BY
GRACE JONES

ILLUSTRATED BY
DRUE RINTOUL

©2017
Roaring Reads
King's Lynn
Norfolk
PE30 4LS

ISBN: 978-1-911419-08-2

A catalogue record for this book
is available from the British Library

CONTENTS

HELLO

It doesn't matter if you are five or ninety-eight.
It doesn't matter if you are from Greece or from Kuwait.
Because when that time comes around, nobody can wait,
to join the festive fun, have a dance and celebrate.

THE EASTER BUNNY

The Easter Bunny,
has an important job to do.
He drops off chocolate eggs,
just for me and you.

He's white and fluffy,
with big, floppy ears.
He comes once a year,
and then he disappears.

Don't forget to thank him,
for your tasty treat,
because the Easter Bunny,
is really very sweet!

Steffi Cavell-Clarke

The Dancing Dragon

There's a huge dragon dancing down the street,
who's stomping and stamping his big, red feet.

Twirling and whirling and swirling he goes,
where the dragon comes from – nobody knows.

Prancing and dancing and twisting his head,
he is the dragon of gold, green and red.

Leaping and twisting and shining in the light,
almost as though he might take-off in flight.

Puffing and blowing and breathing out smoke,
he scares and he frightens the small, young folk.

The dragon told the little ones "Have no fear,
for I am Nian – the dragon of Chinese New Year!"

Grace Jones

DEAR SANTA

Dear Santa,

I know it's very early,
but I didn't want to miss,
the chance for you to get,
my special Christmas list.

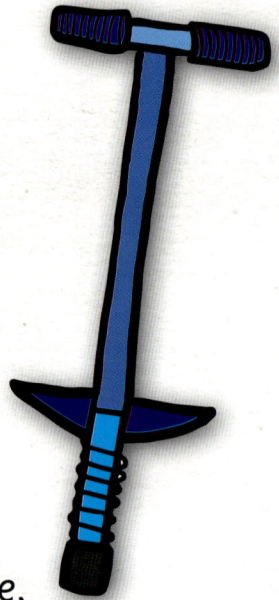

I would like a pogo stick,
maybe in red or blue.
I would also like a skipping rope,
but any one will do.

May I have a talking robot?
And a giant dancing bear?
Maybe you could get me two,
then I wouldn't have to share.

Could I have a cat this year?
Or maybe just a zoo?
How about a rocket ship,
that's shiny and brand new?

That's all I would like for now,
but you can add more too.
I hope you have a good Christmas,
you're the best, thank you!

Steffi Cavell-Clarke

EID AL-FITR

Rumble, grumble,
their stomachs groan.
Burble, gurgle,
their stomachs moan.

The new moon rises,
on the sweet Eid,
bringing many surprises,
and helping those in need.

To fill the hole,
their breakfast waits.
A sugary bowl,
of milk and dates.

Breakfast and lunch,
they chew and burp.
Munch and crunch,
gobble and slurp.

Mike Clark

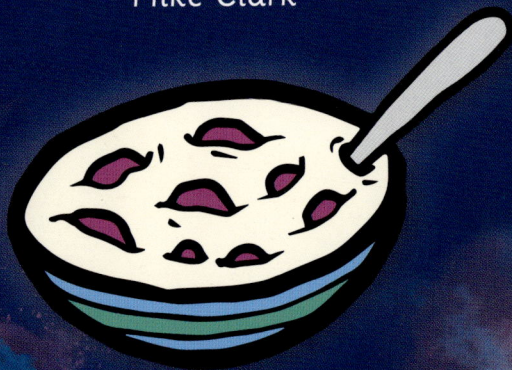

Santa's Sleigh

On Christmas Eve,
you'll hear my ringing sleigh.
Rudolph's red nose,
will guide me on my way.

I'll be dropping off the presents,
to all the girls and boys.
If you've been good this year,
you'll get your favourite toys.

So rest now in your beds,
it's time to go to sleep,
and when you wake up,
you won't have heard a peep.

Kayleigh Briggs

WITCHES' DELIGHT

There's one time of year,
when the moon shines bright,
and the witches come out,
at the stroke of midnight.

These witches are hungry,
they want a tasty bite,
so the best thing to do,
is make them Witches' Delight.

There's a very simple recipe,
that you must follow through,
mix the ingredients together,
to make a tasty brew.

First you need eight worms,
and a cup of green snot,
heat them all together,
and make sure it's extra hot.

Then add a drop of blood,
and mix in a rat's tail,
don't forget the eyes,
and throw in a slimy snail.

Give it a stir and let it cool,
you've made Witches' Delight.
Now leave it out for them to eat,
on a scary Halloween night!

Steffi Cavell-Clarke

HOLI

Paint splat, blue and gold.

Streets filled with people, young and old.

Colourful powder being sold.

Let's buy as much as we can hold.

Paint splat, pink and yellow.

Let's live like there's no tomorrow.

Let's see how much paint we can throw,

on everyone's clothes that we know.

Paint splat, red and green.

More colour than you've ever seen.

More colour than there's ever been.

Don't bother trying to stay clean.

Paint splat, purple and white.

There's no more day, there's no more light.

It seems that this Holi paint fight,

must go on into the night.

Charlie Ogden

FESTIVAL OF LIGHT

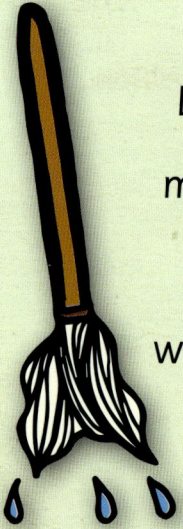

Every single year on this very special day,

my mummy and I go to the temple to pray.

We come back home to clean the house,

washing and scrubbing as quiet as a mouse.

On this very special day we enjoy sweets and treats.

My mummy and I make coconut barfi to eat.

We put bright rangoli patterns outside our door,

hoping that Lakshmi will visit us once more.

Every single year at the festival of light,

my mummy and I light lamps that shine bright.

We light the divas to guide and welcome home,

King Rama and Queen Sita back to their thrones.

On this very special day while I'm lying in my bed,

I hope that we'll have good luck in the year ahead.

My mummy tells me we have nothing to fear,

Lakshmi has visited us so we'll have a good New Year.

Grace Jones

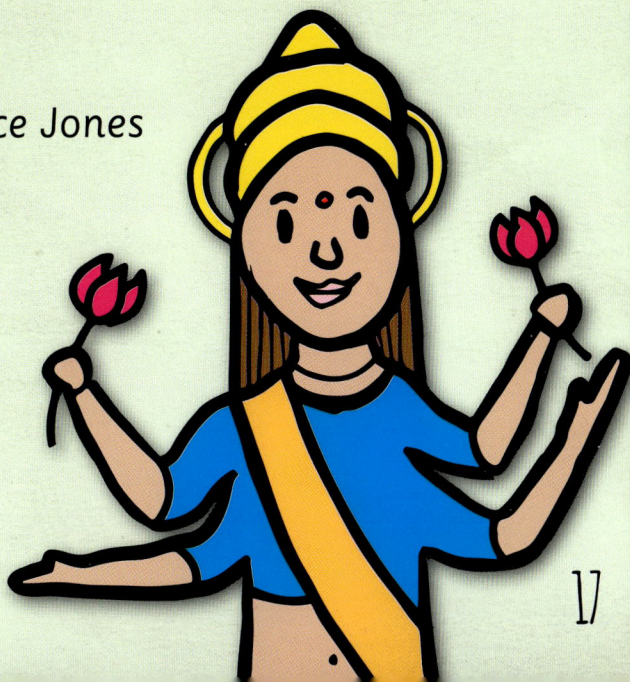

17

HARVEST MOON

It's that time of year again,

when the Harvest Moon shines bright,

so let us gather round,

and celebrate it here tonight.

All the fields are empty,

there's not a crop in sight,

the food is on the table,

so let's take our first bite.

Next grab your Harvest box,

and fill it up with food.

It's time to give it all away,

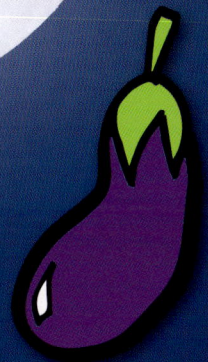

and spread the Harvest mood.

Now the Harvest Moon is gone,

and the night sky looks so clear.

It's time to tend the fields again,

for another year.

Charlie Ogden

ZODIAC TIGER

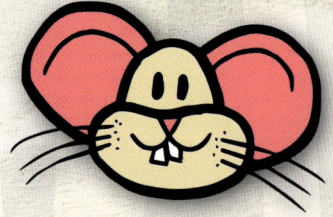

Which animal are you in the Chinese zodiac?

Are you a pig, a dog, a sheep, a rabbit or a rat?

If you are, then I can tell you something for a fact.

They're all rubbish animals – the tiger's where it's at!

Now I can't think of anything that would be worse,

than being born in the year of the ox or the horse.

Except maybe a visit to a dentist or a nurse,

or waking up an angry, sleeping tiger, of course.

People born as tigers make the best queens and kings,

they're always very kind and they aren't scared of a thing.

Monkeys swing, snakes sting and roosters have their wings,

but none of them would win against a tiger in the ring.

There is one zodiac animal that makes tigers go pale.

It has a giant tail and teeth as sharp as nails.

Some people even say that it is bigger than a whale,

but I don't believe in dragons – they're just scary fairy tales.

Charlie Ogden

HANUKKAH

Spin and spin, the driedal goes,

where it will land, nobody knows.

Sweets, more sweets, are the prize.

Chocolate coins were in their eyes.

Whirl and whirl the toy twirled.

A game played around the world.

Spin and spin, the driedal goes,

where it will land, nobody knows.

Clicker, clacker, it begins to slow,

as the grin of a child begins to grow.

"Lucky, very lucky!" the parents would call,

after their child had won them all.

Mike Clark

GOODBYE

The festival has ended, now no one shouts or cheers.
The food has all been eaten and the tables have been cleared.
The town's completely silent, there's no music to hear,
but the festive celebrations will be back again next year!

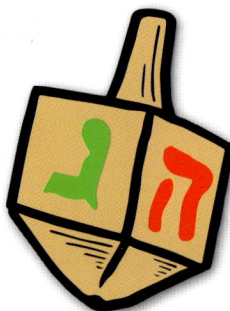